www.finishinglinepress.com

An Ode to Friendship

poems by

Robert Simon

Finishing Line Press
Georgetown, Kentucky

An Ode to Friendship

ACKNOWLEDGMENTS

To my good friends Alicia, Jaime, and João, who brought me back from the brink;
to my friends and fellow oboists Christina, Emily, and Savannah, whose wisdom
has touched my spirit; to my friend Sofia, who in her courage and strength is the
inspiration for this work; to Laurenz, rock of the ages; to Meghan, a friend who
is always there for me; to Eli, friend and videographer; to Federica and Luc, my
professional life givers; to Erik, lifetime learner and best friend from afar; to Chris,
a poet, friend, and scholar; to Audrey, on whose shoulder I know I can always find
support; to Alan, who catches me at the frontier; to Wayne, strength incarnate; to
Debra, friend and teacher, for letting me cry in your office; to Amanda, a friend
whose presence keeps my spirit healthy; to Izara, mi alma gemela; to Helena, my
co-parent and always a best friend; to Sophia, my daughter and whole heart; and
to all the friends who keep us from falling.

This is a story of opening, of friendship, failure, crisis, and redemption. I love
everyone who appears here for a variety of reasons, many of them sublime as the
sun and as fragile as the petals of the Edelweiss. It is also a story of music and
peace. I hope it brings you meaning in hard times.

Publisher: Leah Huete de Maines
Editor: Christen Kincaid
Cover Art: Robert Simon
Author Photo: Kennesaw State University Photography
Cover Design: Elizabeth Maines McCleavy

Order online: www.finishinglinepress.com
also available on amazon.com

Author inquiries and mail orders:
Finishing Line Press
P. O. Box 1626
Georgetown, Kentucky 40324
U. S. A.

Table of Contents

Acordar:

The Awakening 1

Saudades:

About a Friend 5

New Friendship (to Sofia) 6

Ladybug 7

Tornado (on forgiveness, for the self and for others) 8

Leaving March Behind (a poem of atonement and healing) 9

Realidades:

Midnight Ride (to João) 13

McDonalds (to Alicia and Jaime) 14

Bb Major (to Christina and Savannah) 15

Ellipsis (to Meghan) 16

Sacrifice of the wall 17

Reprieve 18

The Talk 19

Cenas de amizade:

Videography (to Eli) 23

The Mountain (to Laurenz) 24

Keep Calm (to Federica and Luc) 25

Recital (to Emily) 26

Direction (to Debra) 27

Shoulder (to Audrey) 28

Redaction (to Alan) 29

Firehose (To Wayne) 30

Evening Stroll (to Amanda) 31

Sua (to Izara)...32

Papéis Avulsos (to David) 33

Telephone (to Erik and Chris)...34

O amanhã:

To Be Your Friend (to all those who keep us from falling)...........37

What I always say to death 38

Recital (or an apology for my mistake) 39

Sit with Me...40

Summer Breeze...41

Mosquitos 42

Panther..43

Concern for a Friend..44

Epílogo:

The End..47

Divorce...48

The Gap..49

How Sophia Saved a Mouse 50

Two Friends (to my daughter and her longtime friend) 51

Notes on the Author..53

Acordar

The Awakening:

Daylight means so many different things now.

Streams of dark yellow almost invisible through branches
Joining and splitting, dew of gods over pollen and soot
The Db minor arpeggio drags against a backdrop of blue

White, thin curtains contain only the day's earthen shadow
A lighter brown, almost grey, hard light and tears
Caress my cheeks at the sight, your voice a longing lost

A dune of moving sounds ease the river's flow,
There's no stopping it now, no wish to fight
Streams of clear salt embedded in joy.

To step out means so many different things now.

27/III/2019

Saudades

About a Friend:

All I ask is to be your friend,
No tricks, no cajoling, no lies.

A breeze through the leaves would suffice
If it meant that your power could shine.

All I ask, to be fair, is to say hello
When passing by, and maybe a word or two
About an instrument's glare or about the sky.

A breeze through the leaves would suffice
When it means that your power will shine.

This is all I ask, to be your friend.

28/III/2019

New Friendship (to Sofia):

To break this world's monotony
you've come to end this silent hypocrisy.

Yours is the face the sailor longs to see
after a long and desperate voyage home;
in your eyes, what longing longs to be.

The word from your lips, a chorale
tuned to distant, radiant shores, the work of seraphim,
or everything the dreamer yearns to dream.

Each strand of hair a bedrock of blackened waves
that flow across a tale of wanting cherubim,
the cry of pearls across a great, divided sky,
an ocean of pinhais in furthest memory.

You are who the weary traveler longs to see,
to break the world's monotony
and take back all that beauty should ever be.

4-8 March 2019

Ladybug:

A symphony, whole
and brassy, alive and
so like the storm breeze outside,
you could hear it only when the
gray door opened to that brilliant sky,

       something from Bach or
       Wagner, a sensual
       heart unfurled,

and among the tremulous leaves,
branches fallen to your Dorian majesty,
She came to rest on your hand.

Black and red, seeking shelter
from the gargantuan movement of that quicksilver gust of divine breath
She came to rest with you.

It was then you said she would give you luck;
how funny and wondrous such innocent interludes can be
for a ladybug and someone like me.

14 March 2019

Tornado (on forgiveness, for the self and for others):

Our house, our qalb, was spared
the power of nature's tornado,
ever moving, lovely, unstoppable,
but wise about the perils
of letting the land overwhelm it.

Letting assumption aside and
taking a thoughtful path,
in my own garden and yours,
our house, our qalb, was yet again spared
the power of the wondrous tornado.

III/2019

Leaving March Behind (a poem of atonement and healing):

I am so happy we find ourselves today,
The world has no more shores or longing,
Safe haven is in all things and everywhere.

The ocean mist tastes of calm, morning splendour;
All the Seraphim have gone to rest and breathe easy
In the deepest moments of these open, Kaddish eyes.

Your courage has shown in everything,
I'm inspired beyond belief;
In friendship, then, we walk along
The path of ship and sea,
A tale of all that could be.

1/IV/2019

Realidades

Midnight Ride (to João):

Only a phone call away
We spent two hours
Between sobbing and self-deprecation

You said I could see the problem
And knew what I had to do
To fix it, and yes, it worked

White walls unfinished, all my fault,
Stabbing at my injured fleshy mind
All my fault, six years, seven,

Between sobbing and a phone at fifty percent
You told me how much I matter

We spent two hours, all my fault,
To fix it, and yes, it worked,

Grey chipped concrete floor
In a house we could afford and
The stabbing at my soul

You brought me from that place,
I can never thank you enough.

III/2019

McDonalds (to Alicia and Jaime):

You took my hand
Which you'd never done before

And made peace with my eyes
Before madness and tears could come out

Your words set a path of light,
This first step home

III/2019

Bb Major (to Christina and Savannah):

Notes of counsel, faith,
Healing words from cane-covered desks,
The flesh of feeling in sonorous airs;

Only scales matter now, distant shores
Seem octaves apart, the space between
Two sides of scraped cane.

Words to heal what flesh wounds turn sour
With time or silence, your meaning
Tempered only by the short time left.

I cannot thank you enough.

III/2019

Ellipsis (for Meghan):

The usual period doesn't go there -
It must be the year of your birth
That makes the learned rules of English girth
A weight from your adulty air

And when you need words of support
You can't just let into the topic
But rather, keep in your pocket
Until with permission, and then you report

Yet darker days may ask of us
A deal of lesser-known acronyms –
A place for you and me to trust
Our room of secret homonyms

So thanks to you I'll never stray from right
And joy in friendship, Messenger's delight

21/VIII/2019

Sacrifice of the wall:

I spoke to you in cautious tones,
Oh mural of safety and pain;

You answered me quickly and sadly,
Now butterfly in a sudden breeze;

This room is yours, thanks to the peacemakers
Of the madness that held you to me.

Sitting up, holding back no arrows,
Arrows tipped with petals of fresh tulip and juniper,

This room will be happy and still,
Thanks to your sacrifice and those constant, waiting words.

28/III/2019

Reprieve:

The Lacrymosa began,

A total lack of dissonance coupled with power chords
And a string section begging for a moment to breathe.

Deus ille, the power of Rome upon us, *and then an ounce of pain*,
Reading along in vain while tears keep us facing forward.

Eyes bound to pages of musical text, Mozart's masterwork,
The one that killed him, *Deus ille, in excelsis, semini ejus.*

It didn't matter anyway, this lovely minor chord in grandeur and ecstasy;
What the heart needed at that moment was the anodyne of its subtle reprieve.

28/III/2019

The Talk (for Helena):

You sat up when I told you
It didn't matter anymore
All the roses in the world
Could never make up for those words.

You leaned back when you heard
My voice unable to make it through
The cascade from my eyes, salted
And desperate, wanting your words.

You made sure I knew you listened
Through joy and pain, the other seraphim,
And told me yes and I'm sorry.

You will never know how that new friend
In her honesty and courage inspired me
To give you a chance and to love you again.

III/2019

Cenas de amizade

Videography (to Eli):

The second stanza vanished
Among people walking in front,

Camera rolling onto bags and feet
Flashing in and out of view,

Runners and amateurs around us;
Until, at the end of all things,

Your perfect angle shown clearly
Captured this lost fado's final tune.

30/III/2019

The Mountain (to Laurenz):

To walk or sprint the hill
Would be decision's fame,
And there a guiding will
Could aid mine to remain

A spirit whose fiery strength
No mount domesticate,
Yet words have shorter length
When time and space debate;

So as the instrument
Her lower voice I play,
Becomes a conduit
For this my soul to say

I cannot sprint the hill,
But walk it I shall try
With dear friends lending will
And faith my destiny decide.

VIII/2019

Keep Calm (to Federica and Luc):

When the afternoon turns raw
And all the trees go bare
You make the world take stock of it
And thus, the mind, aware.

III/2019

Recital (to Emily):

Even when reeds as dry as mine
Could hold the tune no more,
You kept to our consistency
And never lost the shore.

19/III/2019

Direction (to Debra):

True story, a man
Once joined the band
And asked to see
About a thing,

The director said yes,
And then he went
To her office and told
A tale of woe,

Old worries would flow
From eyes too hurt
To speak in words
Of logic or mirth

And she took his hand
(metaphorically, of course)
And gave advice
To calm the man

And when he left
He knew he'd found
A spirit so pure
His heart burst out.

VIII/2019

Shoulder (to Audrey):

Érase una vez,
No one saw what happened
That day,
When it all came down and somehow
I stayed,
No one asked why they just thought
Me habías consolado
When really I was ready to stop

Érase una vez
Yesterday,
Las hojas mecían entre sus robles
Y me miraste
And we walked like an old shoelace
Atados en su felicidad
And then we saw the crowd disperse
And they stopped

An open door, a window of all to be,
The tale of how words travel beyond the sea.

VIII/2019

Redaction (to Alan):

A carefully set table
Brown wood and red cloth
To house the visitors your visitors have brought

Wine among the various dishes
Blue liquor, nameless when finished
And set apart, like a used cocoon

A Battlefield, Earth would understand
The very driven wish to see
A carefully set table, your eyes on them and me

IX/2019

Firehose (to Wayne):

You tried to stand alone again,
Eyes rolling wide and far
From graceful motions deftly made
When moving wasn't so hard

And the only fear was fear itself
And life, an island heart,
As lifting the firehose from the shelf
With the strength of Aries or Mars

Yet now, to stand and fight no longer
Happens in a field of empty carts;
Your love to your left, your friends to your right,
And before you, a galaxy of stars.

IX/2019

Evening Stroll (to Amanda):

To have so much yet want so little,
To see a friend on an evening stroll
With two puppies in tow

To smile and laugh as would lilies
In a field of chrysanthemums
And know not fear or loneliness

To see in every star or treetop
A yoga pose or nightly shift
And aid an older gentleman

To have so much yet want of none,
Your pace and faith and design,
A collage of garden time

IX/2019

Sua:

Tocaste mi brazo derecho con tu mano izquierda,
un gesto de cariño entre las bocas de prietos leones,
no quiero que pienses que al mecer el mío me alejara:

acercaba, de hecho, mi alegre brazo hacia tu mano,
- que en este mundo no hay espacio para los humanos -
la mano del silencio, de todo lo que no hay que decir,
la mano que sujeta la hoja, y la otra que mece
contra el mundo de las multiplicaciones y su devorador ceñir,

tu brazo con mi brazo; tu mano con mi mano,
los ojos como la marcha oscura encendida por la luz,
tu ojo con mi ojo, dos antorchas en la noche oscura de avenidas,
y nuestro añorado abrazo, un corazón que derriba muros.

20 de octubre – 7 de noviembre de 2019

Papéis Avulsos (to David):

Crossing a busy avenue
Rushed, the Beijing way
As would a pile of loose papers
The wind would most happily take

Collecting duly noted credit
Such a coin, a token;
In harmony with pavement
Cracked, yet never broken

You move toward future knowledge
Far from pain and strife.
Your words are those of victory,
A complement to life.

IX/2019

Telephone (to Erik and Chris):

Sharing photos, videos,
Souls and smiles, your
Words only a call away;

- - - - - - - - -

The comfort of your distant voices
With no disdain or criticism
For what are seen as difficult choices
Elucidate my cynicism
And keep the darkness at bay.

III/2019

O amanhã

To Be Your Friend (to all those who keep us from falling):

All I ask is to be your friend;
my mind is here for you to work out problems;
my eyes, to see when pain keeps your vision from sight;
my nose, to help sniff out trouble;
my lips, for words to encourage and nothing more;
my arms, to help you carry a burden or help to solve it;
my shoulder, for you to cry on when things go wrong;
my legs, to walk beside you;
my hopes, that you may fill your heart with all its desires.

This is all I ask, to be your friend.

III/2019

What I always say to death:

When cometh down the looking glass
your favorite voice would shudder make
the strongest of the mammoth placid
spirit fear its soul to take;

Yet, whittling away as time would do
the merriest of bodily rhymes
your face in fear I would not lose
but make to go with you in time.

III/2019

Recital (or an apology for my mistake):

The camera didn't want to work,
An apparatus of ancient times,
The red button glowing in your eyes

So I lifted my own and filmed,
A plan B for success, you'll see,
While I concentrated on our friend's low B

You kept peering back, at first
As though worried I may have kept
Looking at you, perhaps afraid of errors

past, or perhaps because you wished
as I do to go back and not err again.

26/III/2019

Sit with me:

None other but the wispy summer cloud
To take the winter pain away,
When barely turning tree limbs find
Their leaves would wish to stay,

Another time, another place
Perhaps would make this placid day
Seem less a warmer wintry sound
And more a chance to say and say.

V/2019

Summer Breeze:

For any tree to grow
Into its natural place
It need the sun and nutrients
And time and also space

And I, an instant's fire
In summer breeze's shape
Can sit just under memory's shade
And know this friendly grace.

V/2019

Mosquitos:

Never fear the walking dead,
It's been on the air for too long
And lost its fetid, minty smell.

Mosquitos do better; they heave
With the weight of millennia
Basking in a natural niche

Or in a lap around the basement
When Coutier's river of dreams
Makes even more lost the soul,

When evenings fall to reruns
Of tunes I've played over again
Neither aging or putrid, a pause,

And then a smart phone goes off;
It's just a telemarketer pining
To save our mortgage's soul.

1–8/IX/2017

Panther's Meat:

We couldn't avoid all the red veins or chunks of pink
Between the oven-baked thighs, acids and bases,
      The kind no ballad can feign from a sonatina,

An Aria of oven's heat,
The innards of such ossified and fatty parts, some kind
      Of math that we just couldn't reach

So let's hope the cold meat cannot keep me up tonight,
Calculations like meat on a bone, an inside joke
      That no sound or chord can make sense of its light,

Oblivion's simple task, a melody for none to rent,
Pure addition and the flavor of Italy, if not for the French
      Master who'd given it voice, a cry

Of equations we can take, an integral calculus of sound,
Lying in bed with no headache this time
      Or wishes for the morning to take away the ground.

14/IX/2017–18/IX/2017

Concern for a Friend:

We stay up late to wonder
If each word which has passed
Through worried lips may find
Its proper meaning, first or last

And never should we know
If any phrase or peep
Shall take us from our madness –
Allow our minds to sleep.

V/2019

Epílogo

The End:

A letter of good wishes sent
from limb to limb, yellow bees surge
and nature's greeting made and bent

Yet no more word from busy hands
where Cherubim no longer stand
but only silence would silence purge.

And then a feeling, like tendon-laden cuts
of some unfinished sonnet, and in a word,
I thought our feet here solidly stood.

I thought we were past this place
I thought we could talk openly
in this space as though the trees
themselves had opened their branches
and shown the voice of their flowing sap.

I thought we were beyond the past and its fear,
beyond irrational judgment, beyond making
one or the other a last-minute option, clear
only if real friends aren't around to hear or if
no other correspondence would be for the taking

An unopened letter, then, sent without reply,
the trees have closed their leaves, the sap has dried,
the bees don't even care for their good-bye.

23 July 2019

Divorce:

The flowers had long wilted,
Brought home from some meeting
There are so many from what I gather

Petals argued over, should they turn
Red or yellow or an urn of brown
Or maybe we should leave enough alone

Underneath the worn shadow the stalks remain,
It's why we ended our talk and marriage
With a hug and thoughts about meditation

25 February, 2020

The Gap:

Rows of dresses and pants, some yellow or blue, and
Jeggings all around a sea of empty space,

My daughter pulled out a lightly colored piece and
Asked to try it on. Of course I acquiesced.

As she closed the door in the centrally located dressing rooms,
Two young women loosed their ideas into the unsuspecting air.

One asked if her friend was dating that guy, the friend gasped,
No, he's just a friend, a good friend, and the other said, of course,

In the voice of a sailor who thought he saw his beloved land
As the Sirens moved in to greet them. This is the problem,

In a purer, more innocent form, when you're young.

29/III/2019

How Sophia Saved a Mouse:

As it fell, she spoke
In words of pain;
Her jaw bleeding
And face in rain.

As it fell, she cried
In words of love and fear,
Her jaw to speak the words
that only I could hear.

As it fell, the mouse
Upon the trap she cried,
His hands, so strong, so large
That even his heart died.

As it fell, and fell it did,
Upon the trap she stayed,
To keep him company, so that
His fears could be assayed.

And at that moment, finally
The mouse knew it was saved.
The little child fell did not
A leap from the trap she made.

And as it fell, that trap, that mane
Upon the face of the father it stayed
And the little girl, eyes held wide
A kiss to her father she gave.

23/II/2009–IX/2019

Two Friends (to my daughter and her longtime friend):

The sun shone bright today.
Pastures of hazy blue and
A cool wind upon canopy pines,
Pinhais are but a memory,
As would be the strands of
Black hair, images scrolled by.

The two friends sit under the shade
Of a neighbor's barren oak,
Lost in conversation and grass grown
Between them. Theirs is tomorrow's
Longing, last breath of summer's delight.

30/III/2019

Notes on the Author:

Robert Simon holds the title of Professor of Spanish and Portuguese at Kennesaw State University. His publications include: *From Post-Mortem to Post-Mystic: Blanca Andreu, Galicia, and the New Iberian Mysticism (2019), To A Nação, with Love: The Politics of Language through Angolan Poetry* (2017), *The Modern, the Postmodern, and the Fact of Transition: The Paradigm Shift through Peninsular Literatures* (2011), and *Understanding the Portuguese Poet Joaquim Pessoa, 1942-2007: A Study in Iberian Cultural Hybridity* (2008), along with journal articles and book chapters discussing transnational mystical tendencies between Angola, Portugal, and Spain. He has also published several collections of poetry, including *Poems from an Airplane and Graveyard* (2007), *The Traveler / el viajero / o Viajante* (2010), and *Poems of a Turning Professor: A Collection in Two Epochs and Five Parts* (2015). The verses contained in these works express a wish to find a deeper, loving connection with others through themes of love, loss, redemption, and the triumph of the sublime. Robert also moonlights as an oboist and is currently studying Oboe Performance part time.